Get into Science

SOLID, LIQUID OR GAS?

Jane Lacey and Sernur Isik

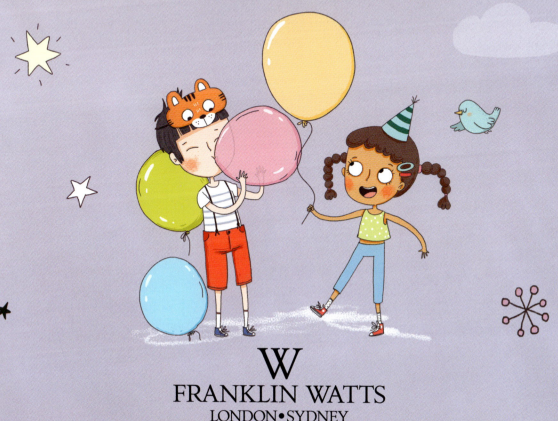

W

FRANKLIN WATTS

LONDON • SYDNEY

Franklin Watts
First published in Great Britain in 2020 by The Watts Publishing Group

Copyright © The Watts Publishing Group, 2020

Credits
Design and project management: Raspberry Books
Art Direction: Sidonie Beresford-Browne
Designer: Kathryn Davies
Consultant: Sally Nankivell-Aston
Illustrations: Sernur Isik

HB ISBN: 978 1 4451 6977 4
PB ISBN: 978 1 4451 6978 1

Printed in Dubai

MIX
Paper from
responsible sources
FSC® C104740
FSC
www.fsc.org

Franklin Watts
An imprint of
Hachette Children's Group
Part of The Watts Publishing Group
Carmelite House
50 Victoria Embankment
London EC4Y 0DZ

An Hachette UK Company
www.hachette.co.uk

www.franklinwatts.co.uk

CONTENTS

VROOOM!!

USEFUL MATERIALS

The things we use and see around us are made of all kinds of different materials.

Bricks, metal and glass are all materials that are good for building. They are all solids.

Can you spot bricks, metal and glass in this building? How has each one been used?

VROOOM!!

THINK ABOUT IT!

What might happen if you built a real house out of cotton wool, string and cardboard?

Cardboard, string, Plasticine and cotton wool are not good for making real buildings. But they are very useful materials. What can you use them for?

The pictures will give you some ideas.

 TRY IT OUT!

Look at some of the things around you, such as a carpet, a door or a spoon. Feel them as well. Do you know what materials they are made from?

ROAR!

5

POURING

The things we use and see around us are made of all kinds of different materials.

Oil, washing-up liquid, honey and water are different kinds of liquid. Liquids can be poured.

Oil

Honey

Washing-up liquid

👋 TRY IT OUT!

Find four bowls and try pouring oil, washing-up liquid, honey and water into them.
Which one pours very slowly? What happens to the liquid in the bowl? Which liquid would you use to fill a paddling pool?

Liquid does not have a shape of its own.

Look what happens when the same amount of water is poured into these different shaped containers.

The water fills up the space and becomes the same shape as the container.

💡 **THINK ABOUT IT!**

Why do you think we usually keep liquids in containers? What other liquids can you think of?

Salt and flour are not liquids but they can be poured because they are made up of thousands of tiny grains.

💡 **THINK ABOUT IT!**

You can pour salt into a pile. Can you pour water into a pile too?

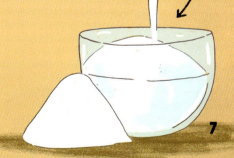

GAS

Did you know that air is a kind of gas? We can't see it but it is all around us.

You breathe air in and out of your lungs.

This balloon is filled with a kind of gas called helium. Helium is lighter than air, so the balloon floats upwards.

TRY IT OUT!

Blow into a balloon.
You can see the air you breathe filling out the balloon. Let the air escape and feel it rushing out of the balloon.

WATER

Water is a very important liquid. We need water to drink to stay healthy and to wash in to keep clean.

THINK ABOUT IT!

Why do boats need water?
Why do firefighters need water?
What other ways do we use water?

Plants need water to grow.

When water is heated up it becomes steam. **Steam is a gas.**

Water is not always a liquid. When it is cooled and freezes, it becomes ice. **Ice is a solid.**

An iceberg is a gigantic block of frozen water. When the sun warms it, the ice melts back into water again and mixes with the sea.

LOOK AGAIN!

Find some solid materials on page 4. Find some liquids on page 6. Find some gases on pages 8 and 9.

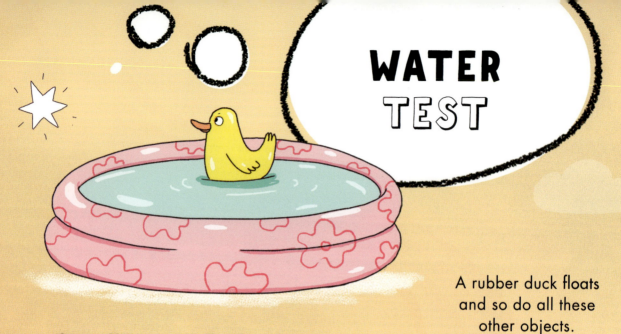

WATER TEST

Some things will float and some will sink when you put them in water.

A rubber duck floats and so do all these other objects.

Marbles, a spoon and a pebble sink.

Look at the different objects on this page. Do you think they are heavy or light? Do you know what they are made of?

 TRY IT OUT!

Collect some objects together. Guess whether the objects will float or sink. Put them in a bowl of water to see if you were right.

When you put some materials in water, they soak up the water and feel soggy.

Other materials don't soak up water at all. **They are waterproof.**

✋ TRY IT OUT!

Find some brown paper, some plastic, a sponge and some wool.
Feel them. Then guess what will happen when you put them in the water.
Which ones will soak up water? Try it out to see if you were right.

MELTING

Butter, chocolate and a wax candle are all solid.

When they are heated, they melt and become liquid.

They become solid again when they cool down.

✋ TRY IT OUT!

Ask an adult to help you melt some chocolate in a bowl over a saucepan of simmering water. Pour the melted chocolate into pastry cutters. When the chocolate cools, it will set into new shapes.

Plastic melts and becomes soft and runny when it is heated.

Melted plastic can be poured into a mould. When it cools down, it sets into the shape of the mould.

Look around you to find some things like these that are made of moulded plastic.

Metal melts when it is heated to a very high temperature. Molten metal is poured into a mould to make a metal toy truck like this.

CHANGING SHAPES

Clay is a kind of mud. You can squash, press and roll it into new shapes.

When clay is fired in a kiln, it dries out and becomes hard.

You can't change the shape of a fired pot – **unless you smash it!**

Pastry dough is soft and can be made into new shapes. When pastry is cooked, it hardens and becomes good to eat!

🐚 LOOK AGAIN!

Look again at page 15. What happens to metal and plastic when they are heated?

You can curl, twist and bend wire. It is good for making models because it will stay in its new shape.

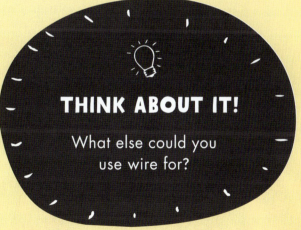

THINK ABOUT IT!

What else could you use wire for?

Thin sheets of metal can be cut, hammered and pressed into new shapes.

DISSOLVING

If you look at salt and sugar through a magnifying glass, you will see hundreds of tiny crystals.

Salt and sugar crystals dissolve when they are mixed with water and make a solution.

👋 TRY IT OUT!

Mix a dessert-spoonful of sugar in half a glass of warm water. Keep stirring until the **sugar disappears.** Dip your finger in the solution you have made and taste it. You can't see the sugar but you can taste that it is still there.

If you mix cooking oil with water it breaks up. It will not dissolve however hard you stir.

✋ TRY IT OUT!

Mix a dessert-spoonful of instant coffee, tea leaves and jam in separate jars of warm water. Do any of them seem to 'disappear' like sugar? What happens to the colour of the water? Which one will not dissolve?

Tea leaves

Jam

Instant coffee

PAPER

Did you know that paper is made from tiny pieces of wood mixed with water to make wood pulp?

Brown bag

The pulp is squeezed out and rolled into sheets of paper.

Kitchen roll

Writing paper

Wrapping paper

✋ TRY IT OUT!

Collect different kinds of paper.
Feel them. Try writing on them, tearing, folding and cutting them. Which one is best for cutting? Which ones tear easily?

Which paper on the opposite page would you use to write a letter?

Which paper would you use to wrap a box of chocolates?

Which paper would be good for mopping up spilt milk?

Which paper item could you use to hold your sandwiches?

THINK ABOUT IT!

Paper is used in hundreds of different ways. How many ways of using paper can you think of?

WHAT
MATERIAL?

What do you think the girl's chair, the baby's bowl and cup, the pan and the window panes are made of?

Can you think why they are made of each type of material?

Look at the opposite page to help you work out the answers.

Metal is strong and does not burn easily.

Wood can be cut and carved. It is strong but it burns easily.

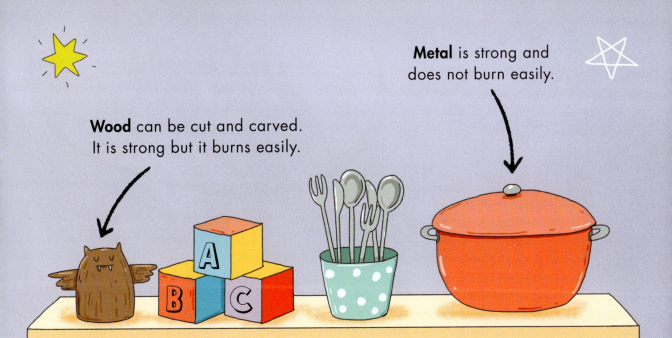

Plastic is tough and light. It can be moulded into different shapes.

You can see through **glass** and it breaks easily.

THINK ABOUT IT!

Glass would not be a good material for making a cup for a baby. Why not? Could a saucepan be made of wood?

NATURAL or MADE?

Some of the materials we use are natural. They come from animals, plants and from the ground.

Wood comes from trees, the biggest plants of all.

Wool comes from a sheep's soft coat.

Gold is buried in some rocks.

Marble is a kind of rock.

LOOK AGAIN!

Look again at page 16 to find another natural material.

Natural materials can be used to make different kinds of materials.

Oil from deep under the ground is used to make material called nylon, used to make clothing.

Sand is one of the materials used to make glass.

🐄 LOOK AGAIN!

Look again at page 23 to find another made material.

25

USEFUL WORDS

AIR

Air is a kind of gas. We can't see it but it is all around us. People, animals and plants all need air to live.

CRYSTALS

Some solids are made up of flat-sided shapes called crystals. Tiny grains of sugar and salt are crystals.

DISSOLVE

When a solid mixes in with water and seems to disappear, we say it dissolves.

FLOAT

Boats float on water. Balloons can float in air. They do not sink under the water or down to the ground.

FREEZE

When water is cooled and turns into ice, we say it freezes.

FUEL

Fuel, such as oil, is something we burn to make energy.

GAS

The air around us is a kind of gas, so is steam from boiling water. A gas does not have a shape of its own.

KILN

A kiln is a type of oven where clay pots are dried out, or fired, at very high temperatures.

LIQUID

Water, milk and oil are all kinds of liquid. A liquid can be poured and it does not have a shape of its own.

MADE

Some materials we use, such as plastic and paper, are made by people. We call them made materials.

MATERIALS

Wood, glass and paper are all different materials. Materials are what things are made of.

MELT

When a solid is heated and turns into a liquid, we say it melts.

MOLTEN

When something has been melted by very great heat and becomes a liquid, we say it is molten.

MOULD

A mould is a hollow shape which is used to give its shape to something, such as plastic.

NATURAL

A plant, an insect and a rock have not been made by people. They are all natural.

PULP

Pulp is a slushy mixture of tiny pieces of wood and water used to make paper.

SHAPE

Every solid object has it own shape. A pencil is a long, thin shape and a ball is a round shape.

SINK

Some things, such as a rock or a coin, will not float on water. They sink down into it.

SOLID

Solid things are neither liquid nor gas. They have shape of their own.

SOLUTION

When some crystals, such as sugar and salt, are mixed with water, they dissolve and make a solution.

WATERPROOF

Some materials are waterproof. When they are put in water, they do not soak it up at all.

QUIZ

Now it's time to see how much you have learned. Try out this quick quiz to test your knowledge.

 Which of these is a solid?

a) Honey
b) Air
c) Brick

 Which of these is a liquid?

a) Honey
b) Air
c) Brick

 Which of these is a gas?

a) Honey
b) Air
c) Brick

 Which of these solid materials would be good for building a house?

a) Cotton wool
b) Bricks
c) String

 What happens when water is cooled and frozen?

a) It becomes ice
b) It becomes jelly
c) It becomes air

 Which of these will float in water?

a) A spoon
b) A rubber duck
c) A pebble

7 Which of these will dissolve in water to make a solution?

a) Glass
b) Metal
c) Sugar

8 Which of these is usually mixed to make paper?

a) Water and wood
b) Water and metal
c) Water and glass

9 Why is glass a good choice for a window?

a) Because it burns easily
b) Because it is soft
c) Because you can see through it

10 Which of these is a natural material (from plants, animals or the ground)?

a) Wood
b) Glass
c) Plastic

ANSWERS

1) Brick
2) Honey
3) Air
4) Bricks
5) It becomes ice
6) A rubber duck
7) Sugar
8) Water and wood
9) Because you can see through it
10) Wood

29

FURTHER INFORMATION

BOOKS TO READ

- *Science in Action: How things work: Materials* by Anna Claybourne (QED 2018)
- *Science in a Flash: States of Matter* by Georgie Amson-Bradshaw (Franklin Watts 2018)
- *Moving up with Science: Matter* by Peter Riley (Franklin Watts 2016)

WEBSITES TO VISIT

- **Go to BBC Bitesize: What are the states of matter?** for an overview on this topic. www.bbc.co.uk/bitesize/topics/zkgg87h/articles/zsgwwxs
- **DK Find Out: Solids, Liquids and Gases** has in-depth information about the properties of matter all around us. www.dkfindout.com/uk/science/solids-liquids-and-gases

ATTRACTIONS TO EXPLORE

Head over to **Techniquest** in Cardiff to explore properties of matter in science activities and experiments. Visit the **Aberdeen Science Centre** for hands-on experience with all kinds of materials. Pop in to **We the Curious** in Bristol, an interactive science and arts education centre, to complete lots of experiments about our world.

NOTE TO PARENTS AND TEACHERS

Every effort has been made by the publisher to ensure that these websites contain no inappropriate or offensive material. However, because of the nature of the Internet, it is impossible to guarantee that the content of these sites will not be altered. We strongly advise that Internet access is supervised by a responsible adult.

ABOUT THIS BOOK

Children are natural scientists. They learn by touching, feeling, noticing, asking questions and trying things out for themselves. The books in the *Get Into Science!* series are designed for the way children learn. Familiar objects are used as starting points for further learning. *Solid, Liquid or Gas?* starts with building bricks and explores materials.

Each double page spread introduces a new topic, such as liquids. Information is given, questions asked and activities suggested that encourage children to make discoveries and develop new ideas for themselves. Look out for these panels throughout the book:

TRY IT OUT! indicates a simple activity, using safe materials, that proves or explores a point.

THINK ABOUT IT! indicates a question inspired by the information on the page but which points the reader to areas not covered by the book.

LOOK AGAIN introduces a cross-referencing activity which links themes and facts through the book.

Encourage children not to take the familiar world for granted. Point things out, ask questions and enjoy making scientific discoveries together.

INDEX

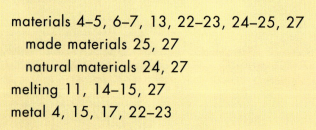

Forces Around Us

- Falling down
- Heavy or light
- What is a force?
- Standing firm
- Push and pull
- Press
- Squashes and stretch
- Stop and start
- Rubbing together
- Drag
- Magnetism

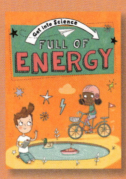

Full of Energy

- Working hard
- Feeling hungry
- Animal energy
- Plant energy
- Full of energy
- Changing energy
- Electricity
- Switch it on
- Keeping warm
- Moving along
- Sun, wind and water

Light and Dark

- Light and dark
- Daylight
- Darkness
- Casting shadows
- Seeing
- Reflection
- Shining through
- Bigger and smaller
- Snapshot
- Rainbows
- A colourful world

Machines We Use

- Rolling along
- Machines
- Wheels
- Wheels with teeth
- Pulleys
- Levers
- More levers
- Hinges
- Balancing
- Slopes and screws
- Making things go

Solid, Liquid or Gas?

- Useful materials
- Pouring
- Gas
- Water
- Water test
- Melting
- Changing shapes
- Dissolving
- Paper
- What material?
- Natural or made?

The Five Senses

- The five senses
- Seeing
- Two eyes
- Hearing
- Listen to this!
- Touch
- Smell
- Paper
- Sniffing out
- Taste
- Keeping safe

Time

- What's the time?
- Time passing
- Day and night
- Measuring time
- Counting the hours
- What's the date?
- A year
- Seasons
- Natural clocks
- Always changing
- Fast and slow

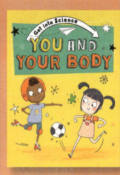

You and Your Body

- Name the parts
- You are special
- Making sense
- Eating and drinking
- Keeping healthy
- Skin
- Under the skin
- Breathing
- Pumping blood
- On the Move
- Sleep well

W
FRANKLIN
WATTS